Dr. Richard St

How is it that we Li

and What is the Me

HOW IS IT THAT WE LIVE AFTER DEATH AND WHAT IS THE MEANING OF LIFE

Manuscript of a
Lecture by
Dr. Richard Steinpach
Vienna

STIFTUNG GRALSBOTSCHAFT PUBLISHING CO.
STUTTGART

"How is it that we live after death" is the perhaps strange-sounding title of this lecture, for it assumes something which for most people is by no means a certainty, namely that there is a continuation of life after death. There are indeed some people who believe in it, but their ideas about it are widely different; and on closer examination it turns out that often it is only a matter of hope, but not of knowing conviction. On the other hand there are those who want to demonstrate how fearlessly they face the limitation of their existence, and who declare that with death everything is over. Finally, between these two camps also stand the great number of those who, for fear of believing in something which has not yet been sufficiently proved, look upon death as a great unknown, the incomprehensible inevitability of which simply has to be accepted.

But we do not have to remain in this uncertainty! The Truth lies within our immediate reach – if we do not close ourselves to it!

In recent years death has been, so to speak, "re-discovered". A separate science is now concerned with dying, thanatology, derived from the Greek word "thanatos", meaning death. Outstanding among the numerous research workers using exact scientific methods in this connection was the American doctor Raymond Moody, whose book "Life after Life"* has become a best-seller. This surely indicates that people are longing for an answer to this question. But to what extent could the numerous books published on the subject in recent years supply this answer?

Just like other researchers, Dr. Moody has compiled reports of the dying, often among them also reports of those who had been declared clinically dead, and who nevertheless could be brought back to earthly existence. The interesting point here was not this medical happening, but the startling similarity of the experiences which those people had in the interval between life and death. They were persons of various levels of education and social status; some lived in the country, some in cities, they were of different nationality and even from different cultures. They had diverse religious views, suffered from different diseases or injuries, and received different medical treatment. Nevertheless, as they hovered between life and death, they had to pass through almost identical phases. With all of them there was to begin with a new state which Dr. Moody calls "being out of the body". The people questioned found themselves outside their bodies. They saw themselves – or better said this body, with which they no longer identified themselves – lying on the bed or at the place of the accident; they saw the efforts of those around them and heard their words. Those persons who – according to Dr. Moody – "had penetrated more deeply into the realm of death" had the feeling of being drawn through a dark narrow

* Bantam Books, Inc., 666 Fifth Avenue, New York 10019, USA

passage. Then they saw a bright but not blinding light, sensed the nearness of a loving being, and experienced a "playback" of their life. Their concept of time and their knowledge had altered, expanded, and they thought they understood the true connections.

I need not concern myself here with the doubts which were raised over Dr. Moody's report on "Life after Life". Dr. Moody himself has adequately refuted the sceptics. Here something else is to be dealt with: Valuable and important as the research findings of the thanatologists are, still they have only compiled descriptions of experiences. They have not yet explained thereby the process of dying. To understand the significance of this so important turning-point, however, we must after all know how it can happen at all that we go on living after death.

To close this gap is the purpose of this lecture. You shall receive here those explanations that you have not found in any of the books about dying which have been published in recent years. That is to say, only then will you be in a position to understand and fit in the reports compiled by the scientists. For there is nothing sinister or sensational about these reports. They are fragments, instantaneous recordings from a happening which you shall be in a position to survey to a much greater extent. For death too is a completely natural process, which takes its course according to firmly-established, clear and – what seems to us most important – intelligible Laws. –

I should like to say in advance: The explanations which you are to hear are based on the Grail Message, "In the Light of Truth"*, a Work yet to be spoken of. That it bears its title with justification you can already see from the very fact that what is stated in it can for instance explain to us all the processes associated in the widest sense with death.

I therefore invite you first of all to receive without prejudice what I wish to present to you on the subject. When I say "without prejudice" I mean by this: Whenever you read or hear something that seems to you new or startling, you should not immediately protest, saying "that cannot be" or measure it by your own previous conceptions. Rather should you reflect on it and examine what you have heard. But you can and should examine it afterwards by applying it to the facts that are known to us, and to the descriptions put forward.

And finally by this I mean yet something else: We should at last rid ourselves of the habit of regarding what is invisible as incomprehensible or even unnatural. This attitude is quite unjustified. We know only too well how inadequate are our senses. Even infra-red light, ultra-violet light or ultra-sonic sound can no longer be perceived by us. We are constantly surrounded, indeed permeated by waves of the most diverse kinds without noticing it. It would therefore be absurd for man to deny that there are also realities beyond our senses. The very fact that we have such a concept as "the beyond" at all surely means that we are quite aware of the existence of such worlds.

For a better understanding of what is to follow, let us be-

* Verlag der Stiftung Gralsbotschaft, Stuttgart, Germany

gin at once by defining these regions. From now on I shall refer to the earthly as the World of Gross Matter, and to the beyond as the World of Ethereal Matter; but we must be clear that this is only a broad distinction, which for the time being disregards the stages of transition.

The first requirement for further contemplation is that we obtain clarity about ourselves, about the question: What really is man? The recognitions of the Darwinists, neo-Darwinists, the behaviourists and evolutionists are indeed only half-truths, right and wrong at the same time. For they are concerned only with the development of our body and its organs. But the real man is not this body. That would be as though one did not differentiate between the driver of a vehicle and the vehicle itself. For there is certainly within us something which is capable of being conscious of itself, which can think about itself; something which already distinguishes us from the animal. This something can intuitively perceive not only joy and sorrow, love and hate, but also such abstractions as art, beauty, sublimity. And with this expression "intuitively perceive", which seems to offer itself naturally here, we touch precisely upon the actual human within us. This actual humanity is spirit! Its voice, its language, through which it makes itself perceptible to us, is the intuitive perception. It is that welling-up which does not depend on external sensory stimuli, but flows forth spontaneously from the innermost depth of our being.

With this we have indeed found the way to the sensing, to the experiencing of our spirit, but I find it necessary to define this concept still more sharply. Therefore listen to what is said about it in the Grail Message, "In the Light of Truth":

"Spirit is not wit, and not intellect! Nor is spirit acquired knowledge. It is erroneous, therefore to call a person "rich in spirit" because he has studied, read and observed much and knows how to converse well about it. Or because his brilliance expresses itself through original ideas and intellectual wit.

"Spirit is something entirely different. It is an independent consistency, *coming from the world of its homogeneous species, which is different from the part to which the earth and thus the physical body belong. The spiritual world lies higher, it forms the upper and lightest part of Creation . . .*

"Spirit has nothing to do with the earthly intellect, only with the quality which is described as 'deep inner feeling' ('Gemuet'). To be rich in spirit, therefore, is the same as 'having deep inner feelings' ('gemuetvoll'), but not the same as being highly intellectual."

It is a sad indication of the extent to which we have already buried the spirit within us that we are able, as alas so often happens, to confuse it at all with the intellect. The only thing which the intellect can do, namely to connect experiences and information supplied to it, and to draw conclusions from these, can today already be done much better by computers than by us. Indeed the intellect is only an instrument bound to the body, an instrument which is meant to enable the spirit to manifest in accordance with its nature in this earthly world.

Thus our true ego is spirit. It is the only living thing which is within this earthly body, and which keeps it alive as such. But this spirit is not directly inside the body, for its species is too different from that of the earthly body. After all, we know that Nature makes no leaps. The only one it does know is the quantum leap, the joining together of minimal quantities of energy, which however precisely demonstrates the extent to which in the natural happening one building-stone always follows another for progression, by small stages only. Thus the spirit also has next to it finer, lighter, more permeable coverings, coming closer to it in the gradation-order of Creation, and thus also one of ethereal substance. It is this manifestation, the spirit in its ethereal body-covering, which has been seen already by many clairvoyant persons, and to which the concept "soul" – by which unfortunately people usually envisage so little – is applicable. The "soul" therefore is not something independent which exists side by side with the spirit; it is the spirit clothed in ethereal substance.

A positively dramatic account of the existence of such an ethereal body is to be found in the New Testament, according to which after His burial Jesus appeared to Mary Magdalene, and also several times to His disciples. He walked beside them, they spoke with Him, but they did not recognise Him. He entered rooms whose doors were locked – and only when He broke bread with them at the table did they perceive that it was Jesus. This surely testifies quite clearly that He came to them in a different, changed bodily form, in precisely that ethereal body, which they, shaken by the deep experiences arising from the events of the previous days, were enabled to see at that time. Had it been otherwise, they would surely have recognised Him immediately. But Jesus wished by this not only to tell them that HE was risen; HE wished to demonstrate to them that life goes on, not only after a far-off Judgment Day, but immediately after earthly death.

But even this ethereal body just discussed is still too different in nature from the earthly. Therefore between this ethereal soul and the gross material earthly body another necessary transition is inserted, the so-called astral body. It already comes very near to the earthly body in its consistency; the astral body is the direct prototype of the physical body, its model so to speak. It may perhaps seem strange to express it in that way. But we know today that the minutest building-stones of our material substance, the neutrons, protons and electrons, do in fact have such finer prototypes. These are the so-called "sub-atomic particles". A large number of them, becoming ever less material, have already been discovered. And now, please consider: Like all material substance our bodies also consist only of such elementary particles. Is it not then really obvious that the sub-atomic prototypes of these particles must in turn produce a finer form of the body? When moreover we consider that everything which seems to us to be firmly-knit matter – scientifically proved – arises from radiation, from that incomprehensible something which we describe as "cosmic radiation"; that here an unceasing process of alternation is at work, which transforms radiation into particles and particles into radiation, then, ladies and gentlemen, this tells us quite clearly that our whole earthly world is formed, as one might say, from above downwards; it is simply the result of a continuous process of consolidation. The existence of such finer coverings therefore follows directly as the logical consequence of our physical world-picture. How far this world-picture can be expanded beyond the boundary of fixed conceptions can be seen from the mere fact that, for example, only a few decades ago the recognitions of relativity theory, quantum physics, molecular biology or radio-astronomy would have been ridiculed as fantasy, occultism or superstition.

Let us therefore once more hold fast to those three concepts with which we shall have to occupy ourselves in the following: There is on the one hand the gross material earthly body, which is also called the "mortal cloak", after that the astral body, which in its consistency comes very close to it; and finally the spirit in its ethereal body-covering, the so-called soul. Now the soul is connected with the astral body, and thereby also with the physical body, through the "silver cord", which likewise has often been seen by clairvoyant persons. It is a kind of ethereal umbilical cord. In fact it runs into the same place as the gross material navel cord which once connected us with the womb, that is in the solar plexus. This "silver cord" is – on sober consideration – the ethereal manifestation of that "construction-design" which we find again in the umbilical cord familiar to us. It is the channel for the influence of the spirit on the physical body.

You may now want to ask: Where are these various coverings, then? Indeed they are all inside us. Yet because of their different consistency they cannot blend with each other, but only unite. They are pushed into one another like the parts of a collapsible telescope, and they are held in this position, bolted as it were by that tremendous power that holds together everything in Creation, from the greatest to the smallest. This power is radiation. Today we know of course from physics that everything radiates, that the apparent solidity of our material substance is due to nothing other than just this radiation, which magnetically connects the elementary particles.

Ladies and gentlemen, may I remind you in this connection of an old, well-known proverb which says: "Food and drink keep body and soul together." This is mainly taken as a justification of the pleasures of the table. Yet what wisdom, what knowledge of the true connections lies in it! For it is clearly stated here that body and soul are two separate things, that they are only held together, and that for this a certain consistency of the physical body is necessary, the achievement of which simply requires a supply of material nourishment. If it does not receive this nourishment or if it is struck by illness, then it is weakened. But this of necessity means that its radiating-power, its radiation, also becomes weaker.

With this we have arrived at the decisive point. I will now hand you the key to the understanding of that happening with which we are here dealing. I will again do this with words from the Grail Message, "In the Light of Truth", in which we read:

"Thus it happens . . . that the soul must sever itself from a body which has been forcibly destroyed, or from one ruined by disease or weakened by old age, at the very moment when t h i s b o d y, owing to its changed condition, can no longer produce t h a t strength of radiation which brings about such a magnetic attraction-power as is necessary to contribute its share in the firm union between soul and body! This results in earthly death, or the falling back, the falling away of the gross material body from the ethereal covering of the spirit, thus in separation. A process which takes place, in accordance with firmly-established Laws, between two species which only unite at an exactly corresponding degree of heat through the radiation simultaneously produced, but which can never blend, and which fall apart again when one of the two different species can no longer fulfil the condition laid upon it."

Hence soul and body must contribute their share to this radiation-connection. Of course it is generally the earthly body wearing itself out whose radiation diminishes for one of the afore-mentioned reasons; but it can also be that the connection is severed because the radiation of the soul is no longer directed to the earthly body with the necessary strength. These then are cases where a human being, not suffering from any specific disease, departs this life simply because he no longer has any will to live.

But here too there are of course intermediary stages. If someone does not feel well, physically or psychically, are we not inclined to say: "*He is not quite himself*" or: "*He is not in his right mind*"? Surely these phrases quite clearly refer to a loosening of the cohesion necessary for our full strength. Thus we read on in the Work "In the Light of Truth":

"Even when the gross material body is asleep its firm union with the soul is loosened, because during sleep the body produces a different radiation, which does not bind so fast as that required for the firm union. But since the union still exists only a loosening takes place, no separation. This loosening is immediately ended at each awakening."

With this hint on sleep, a bridge is made for our understanding. For here indeed it is a question of an experience which each of us can have every night. Sleep has often been described as the little brother of death. Was this only because in sleep man is removed from active life? Or were not people after all aware of the common cause, based on the Laws of Nature?

Although man is known to spend one third of his life in sleep, science only began to apply itself to research into sleep about two decades ago. The findings of this research are unfortunately still too little known generally. I would therefore like to tell you something about it, because here we already have the first possibility of recognising the rightness of what has just been said.

We know that micro-electric processes are constantly going on in our brain, which can be measured as brain-current on the electro-encephalograph. This brain-current shows up to thirty cycles per second in the waking state. In sleeping persons it drops to half a cycle per second in the course of falling asleep. But at the same time the heartbeat, respiration, blood-pressure and body temperature also diminish. The body economy is maintained only on a "pilot-light". Research has thereby established the outward signs of a weakening of all vital functions, naturally also accompanied by a weakening of the body's radiation, which is dependent on these vital functions. This, however, confirms exactly what you have just heard: For this diminished body-radiation makes possible the loosening of the soul. Before achieving deep sleep some sleeping persons even have the sensation that they are falling – they jump. It is the moment when the soul rises out of the hitherto firm radiation-connection.

Only after reaching deep sleep does the phase of eventful dreaming begin. As sleep research has discovered, it can never be attained while standing or sitting. For this the body needs a horizontal support, which allows a fully-relaxed repose. Muscle and tendon reflexes have now ceased, so that occasionally even the chin drops and the person snores. Thus the body lies there free of tension, like the covering of a ball from which the air has escaped. What more do we need by way of proof that here the carrying-animating support is lacking, and therefore is obviously of a different species from this earthly body?

But while the body is thus relaxed we dream. Sleep research has established that all human beings dream every night. Why we only sometimes remember this can indeed be easily explained, but it would lead us too far from our subject. That a person is dreaming can also be confirmed by the fact that at the same time the eyes move to and fro remarkably quickly behind the lids. This rapid eye-movement, which can be measured on the oculograph, is so characteristic that it has even given a name to this phase of sleep. It is called REM-sleep, which is an abbreviation of "rapid eye-movements".

If the sleepers were awakened during this phase, they confirmed that they had just been having vivid dreams. The eye-movements behind the closed lids corresponded to the content of the dream: If someone had dreamed that he was climbing up a ladder, his eyes would be looking upwards, if he dreamed that he was lifting something from the ground, he would be looking down. But nothing is to be seen through the closed lids of the earthly body. In this way research already gives us proof that after all our ego is something other than this body, and that this ego, the spirit, sees and experiences, in the course of which the eyes of the earthly body follow these impressions only because in sleep the connection of the soul with the body is not yet severed, but only loosened. That these eye-movements take place more rapidly than in a waking state, and are jerky, even indicates to us that the spirit is experiencing a world of higher animation, which the sluggish earthly eye is hardly in a position to follow.

Thus we already find here confirmation of the fact that the change of radiation releases to us a new sphere of experiencing. It already makes possible the loosening of the soul, and the spirit present within this soul then experiences, in a world beyond, that which we describe as dreaming.

If further emphasis is needed that the radiation is decisive for union between soul and body, it can be seen in the following: Sleep research has established that the phase of REM-sleep, that is the stage at which the soul has already loosened itself from the body, can be reached more quickly in a cool room. The reason is obvious: The reduced room-temperature leads to a quicker decline in body-temperature, and therefore to an earlier decrease in its radiation which, as you have heard earlier, is also dependent on a certain degree of heat. Finally we all know also that stage between dreaming and waking when conscious thinking is already beginning to set in, but when we are still unable to move the body. We are just bringing the "soul" near, and as long as the radiation of the body is still not strong enough, the soul simply does not have it fully "in its grip". It is like engaging the clutch in a motor vehicle.

And now, after this first experiment as an example, let us turn to death. When, in the opinion of science, does it take place? The view held today is that brain-death is the decisive sign. By that is understood the cessation of the brain-current on the electro-encephalograph. This is in complete agreement with what sleep-research has established, and at the same time with what we have heard about the magnetic union of body and soul brought about by radiation: The diminishing of the brain-current up to the attainment of deep sleep has led to the loosening of the soul; the cessation of this wave-pattern appears to medical science to be death. But what is the brain-current, other than a measurable vibration peculiar to the body? And vibration in its turn is only a manifestation of radiation, because all radiation appears as vibration, is vibration. If such a vibration is no longer present as measurable, this to the doctor signifies death. Thus you see that science strictly establishes what matters, but it sees only the fact and does not yet recognise its actual significance.

But as can already be ascertained during the gradual attainment of deep sleep, the decline in the body-radiation does not take place suddenly. If we disregard those cases in which the body is destroyed by violence or mutilation, then it is a question of a smooth, gliding process, as if one were slowly and steadily reducing the current of an electro-magnet and finally switching it off. This explains the difficulty in accurately determining the time of death. It was formerly thought that it had set in when the respiration ceases, thereafter, when the heart stops. Now it is assumed that a person is dead when the brain-current stops. But where actually is the end? How is it possible for the "clinically dead" to be able to come back to life?

Let us then take a quick glance in the opposite direction. What happens at entry into earthly life? Here also, the medical world cannot state clearly when human life begins. In connection with the question of abortion particularly, the most diverse opinions have been put forward. Here too the reason lies in the fact that the attracting of the soul through the increasing radiation of the developing earthly body takes place gradually, until the magnetic union holds. The infallible signs of this are the first movements of the child in the womb.

Only now has the soul taken full possession of the body, and is able to move it.

Thus "clinical death" also is only that moment in which the too greatly diminished body-radiation no longer allows the soul still to maintain the bodily functions at a measurable strength. But just as with entry into life the connection with the approaching soul gradually became stronger, so also is its severance not yet finally completed at the point in time which we regard as that of death. –

We have so far discussed the means by which death comes about, namely through the weakening of the radiation-connection. Now let us occupy ourselves with what really happens at death. Again I would like to tell you this in words from the Grail Message, "In the Light of Truth":

"At severance of the soul, this as the mobile part draws the astral body with it away from the physical body. Figuratively speaking: Upon its exit and departure the soul draws the astral body with it out of the physical body. That is how it appears. In reality the soul only pulls it off the physical body, because there was never a fusion but only a sliding into one another, as with a collapsible telescope.

"In so doing the soul does not draw this astral body very far, because it is anchored not only with the soul but also with the physical body; and moreover the soul, from which the actual movement issues, wants to sever itself also from the astral body, and accordingly strives away from it as well.

"Thus after the earthly departure of the soul the astral body

always remains near the physical body. The further the soul moves away, the weaker the astral body also becomes; and the ever-advancing severance of the soul finally brings about the decay and distintegration of the astral body, which in turn immediately brings in its train the decay of the physical body, in the same way as it also influenced its formation. This is the normal process in accordance with the Laws of Creation."

Let me once more summarise this explanation because of its great importance: Through the body-radiation having become too weak, the connection of the telescoped coverings is severed; they are so to speak unbolted. Like a balloon which is no longer tethered, the soul as the lightest part then floats away. But with it the spirit contained in this ethereal covering also moves away. It alone, as the only living thing in man, was in a position to hold together the structure of the body in the astral as well as in the earthly gross-material sphere. If the connection with the spirit is severed, these forms must disintegrate again.

But now, in the passage which I have just read to you, it has been said that this is the normal process in accordance with the Laws of Creation. For the severance of the soul does not always take place so simply. I may remind you that not only is the soul kept within its denser coverings through the mutual radiation, but it has in the already-mentioned "silver cord" a direct lead, a connection to the astral body, and thereby to the physical body. What is decisive for the soul not only to slip out of its body, but to detach itself completely from it, is the condition of the ethereal soul-body and its homogeneous connection-cord, which depends entirely on the spiritual nature of the individual human being.

If through his volition a person has strongly adjusted himself to the earthly, if he did not wish to know anything about a continuing life after death, of an ethereal world in the beyond, then through this, through his own attitude, the connection-cord is very firmly knit, and will be difficult to sever. The severance may then take many days, during which time such a person, because of the density of the connection-cord, must still feel what happens to his physical body, so that he does not necessarily remain insensitive for example to cremation.

On the other hand the connection-cord in the case of a noble spirit striving for the Light, who bears within him the conviction of a continuing life, can very soon become so loose that it no longer acts as a channel for pain, and the dying person is even spared the last physical pains.

You may see from this how immensely important it is to know of these things. Your attitude to the question of death helps to decide how easy or how hard it will one day be for your soul to detach itself from your body. But it also reveals how much harm is caused by the lack of knowledge about the process of dying. Thoughtlessly, post mortem examinations are carried out in hospitals, the supposed corpses are dissected. Even worse: Since the medical world has succeeded in transplanting organs it views the dying as a kind of store for spare parts. Many institutions and persons in public life advocate this, indeed they absolutely consider it a human duty to permit the removal of organs from the discarded body. There is nothing against the well-meaning motive that leads a donor to make such a disposition, although – viewed in a higher sense – it is hardly to the benefit of the one provided for. But every such donor must know what he is thereby taking upon himself. At the time the organ is removed, which as is well-known must take place immediately after the presumed death if the organ is still to be usable, he is by no means "really dead", otherwise the organ could no longer be fit for use. In any case up to that time the connection-cord is not yet completely severed. Where the density of the connection-cord, depending on the nature of the person concerned, is still fitted to act as a channel for pain, such a person will still feel the infringement very perceptibly. It is therefore with good reason that some rites, especially among primitive races, provide for minimum intervals between death and the funeral, or even cremation.

But in the limited continuation of this connection-cord also lies the explanation of how it was that the persons interviewed by the thanatologists, several of whom had indeed already been considered "clinically dead", could return to life. In all these cases the connection-cord simply was not yet severed.

This natural fact also explains the alleged miracle of the waking of the dead, thus also that of Lazarus. In this Creation nothing can take place that would not be in accordance with its Laws. To return to earthly life is always only possible for him whose "line" between spirit and earthly body still exists, thus making re-entry possible. The miraculous in such happenings lies in the to us incomprehensible power which brings about such a return. In the cases reported by Dr. Moody, it was of an other-worldly nature; in the case of Lazarus through Jesus, even of a Divine kind.

Especially from the Biblical accounts of the raising of the dead by Jesus can the increasing distance of the soul from the body be recognised, and the ever greater force that is needed in order to strengthen the radiation-connection again. In the case of the daughter of Jairus, who had just departed this life, Jesus (according to Luke 8, 54) simply says: "Maid, arise"; with the young man of Nain, who is about to be buried, He already becomes more urgent: "Young man, *I say unto thee,* Arise" (Luke 7, 14); finally in the case of Lazarus, who had already been lying in the grave for four days, Jesus *prays,* before crying with a *loud voice:* "Lazarus, come forth" (John 11, 41–43).

In this connection I must yet refer to something which it is extremely important for us all to know and to heed. Namely this: Again and again it happens that near relatives break out into loud lamenting in a death chamber, and try to make the departing one say something further. However understandable this may be from their standpoint, they are thereby unknowingly guilty of a gross lack of consideration for the dying person. For the wish is thus awakened in him to be able still to make himself understood. But he can only make himself understood in an earthly way by means of the physical body from which he is just about to sever himself. His wish now works against this process, for through it he seeks to bind himself again to the earthly. This leads to a renewed densification of the connection-cord, which thereby again becomes more adapted to being a channel for pain. Through such a longing the dying person is thus more firmly bound to the physical body again, and compelled to feel its pains once more. This results in an unintended prolonging of the process of dying, in a death struggle sometimes dragging on for days, because the personal volition of the dying one has interfered with the process. Therefore absolute quiet should reign in a chamber of death, a dignified solemnity in keeping with the important hour.

I believe that no serious-minded person who has grasped what takes place at death can evade the logic of this. For death is nothing but rebirth into a world beyond, from which we came. Let us therefore strive not to make this step hard particularly for a loved one through our grief, which is really selfishness.

And now, after hearing all this, it will be easy for us to understand the experiences of the persons questioned by Dr. Moody. Since to begin with we have also dealt with the subject of sleep, we can undertake to classify these experiences. For they are always to be found in the realm between sleep and death. There are accounts of people who lay seriously ill, and who on the threshold between life and death saw deceased relatives or helpers from the beyond, and spoke with them. Then finally there are the descriptions of those who found themselves already outside their bodies, and of whom some had already been considered "clinically dead". But none of these was really dead, that is, the connection-cord had not yet been severed. It is just through this that these descriptions, as intermediate stages on the way from life to death, complement the picture of that smooth transition of which I have already spoken. For the nightly dream-images still partly superimposed by the impressions of the day, the visions of the beyond by the dangerously ill, the withdrawal from the physical body with the subsequent ever further-reaching experiences of the presumed dead, and finally death, all appear as though arranged in sequence.

Therefore Dr. Moody has also rightly arrived at the conclusion: "In general persons who were 'dead' seem to report more lasting, complete experiences than those who only came close to death, and those who were 'dead' for a longer period go deeper than those who were 'dead' for a short time." But this implies nothing other than: The further the loosening of the soul, and therewith its withdrawal from the physical body, has progressed, the more impressions of the beyond it experiences.

Thus the perceiving of persons who were invisible to others – hence those visions which the dangerously-ill had – is still very close to the experiencing in the beyond of dreaming people. The body-radiation of the seriously ill, however, is already so much diminished that the soul is able to loosen itself even a little more than in dreaming. Therefore it already sees the world of the beyond more clearly, more distinctly, no longer mingled with daytime impressions absorbed by the brain, as is frequently the case with our dreams.

The next perplexingly new experience then is that of the "out-of-the-body state", of no-longer-being-in-the-body. Here the soul, no longer held fast enough by the body-radiation, has already drawn the astral body off the physical body, and the real man, the spirit, now looks through this astral body at the physical body. In this state the persons were able to see what was happening around this physical body, they heard the words of those standing by, indeed they could even recognise their thoughts just before they were uttered. But how is this possible?

Here too it is a matter of something completely natural. Just as in the gross material eyes and the gross material organs of hearing our gross material physical body possesses the sense-organs corresponding to its consistency, so also the astral body and the ethereal body have the particular homogeneous equipment corresponding to them. But it is always our spirit which sees, hears or feels through the sense-organs of the particular outermost covering, thus never the eye or the ear itself. The spirit within the astral body thus perceives through the sense-organs of the latter.

And here we must for once become fundamentally clear as to the real nature of these worlds in the beyond which already begin with the astral plane, as to what makes them different from our world. I have said before that our earthly world is actually only a solidification arising from radiation. But solidification means loss of lightness, mobility, it means becoming more sluggish, heavier. With any earthly substance which melts, vaporises and becomes gaseous, we can observe this as a converse process. Its dematerialisation, the increasing lightness is based on an ever faster movement within its atoms. This movement manifests as vibration. In other words: In the final analysis finer, lighter forms are therefore always only ever faster states of vibration. And now please think of a radio receiver. It comprises different wave-bands: medium waves, short waves, ultra-short waves. If then you switch from one band to the other the set is suddenly able to receive higher frequencies, thus livelier vibrations, which until then were not accessible to it. The reason for this is that it is now tuned in, that is its receiving equipment is homogeneous to these vibrations and can therefore receive them. Thus we too bear within us receiving equipment for different wave-bands in the form of the physical body, the astral body, the soul-body. For this reason the "out-of-the-body state" involves first a "switch-over" to the immediately adjoining wave-band of a higher frequency. But the division here is not so sharp as in a radio-receiver; the transitions are again smooth. Since the astral sphere is still very near to the earthly, the departing one, who gradually begins to change over (let us for the sake of clarity keep to this expression) to the "frequency band" of the other world is at first still able to include both sides in his perceptions. Thus he can recognise the thoughts whose vibrations – that is when they have become so concentrated that they are just about to be uttered – lie within this range, shortly before they are formed into words, and also still see and hear the earthly.

But: He for his part can no longer make himself noticeable. If you have followed the explanations so far it will be clear to you that it simply cannot be otherwise. For the instrument for earthly communication is the earthly body, from which by this time the dying person has already slipped out, and which at this stage he can no longer move. Even the astral body-covering is generally invisible to our gross material eyes, the words he forms with it remain in a sphere of vibration to which our sense-organs are just as unreceptive as they are to the radio or television waves constantly surrounding us. Nor does our earthly body respond to the touch of the astral or even the ethereal body of the departed. This state of being no longer heard, no longer seen, is a painfully distressing experience for one who passes over without knowing about these processes. He sees his relatives mourning and would like to call out to them: "What is the matter with you? I am still alive!" He sees the doctors handling his body and would like to drive them away, but no one takes any notice of him. The ignorant person feels himself to be alive in this intermediate region and yet expelled from all the living. It is an experience of terrifying loneliness.

May you recognise from this how senseless it is to have pushed aside everything connected with dying as though just the most inevitable thing in this earth-life had nothing at all to do with us.

And even now, when people are at last prepared to break the taboo, they are caught at the boundary of what they believe can still be "scientifically" proved. But what matters is to enlighten people unreservedly about everything that takes place at death and behind it, because all this belongs inseparably to the great oneness of our existence.

Surely we shall all have to cross this threshold one day. Is it not better to do this knowingly, instead of being pushed out into the unknown?

But such knowledge is essential for us not only for this hour, which indeed is approaching every one of us, but already beforehand. Thus at funerals people follow a coffin. How few of the so-called mourners remember the deceased with loving thoughts! How much evil or trivial talk often goes on in a funeral procession. If these people knew that the deceased is perhaps still near, that he can hear them, they would behave differently. –

Let us return to Dr. Moody's report on "Life after Life". Many of the persons questioned by him had indeed experienced more than the "out-of-the-body state". Where they "had penetrated more deeply into the realm of death" they had a remarkable experience: They felt as if they were gliding through something dark and narrow, a valley, a dark shaft, a tunnel. Difficult as it is to put an experience in the beyond into earthly word-concepts, those concerned were characteristically agreed in speaking of being "pulled out", or on their return being "drawn in" to earth-life. Here we are therefore already dealing with the next phase, the striving away of the ethereal soul from the astral body, thus the soul's pulling out from the latter. At these moments of transition, of the striving away movement, the spirit can now no longer see through the eyes of the earthly or astral body, nor as yet through those of the ethereal body, which is only about to become free. Therefore the spirit temporarily has the impression of darkness. It is as though one were inside a lift moving between two floors. There we cannot look out either, but must wait until the next floor is reached.

That this next stage which the soul now enters is actually a world of faster vibration is emphasised by an acoustic experience which the persons questioned had while being "pulled out". For they heard a noise, and described it as the booming of a bell, a rushing, a roaring, a bang. Thereafter they found themselves suddenly in the brightness of a new world, the earthly had disappeared from them. Now we know from many earthly phenomena that where two movements of different speed collide, such acoustic effects result. Just think of the uncorking of a champagne bottle, the crack of a whip, or – clearer still – of the boom that arises when a supersonic aircraft breaks the sound barrier. Thus also for the soul, the entry into its new form of existence is like the breaking of a sound barrier. It changes over into a world of faster vibration.

A result of this faster vibration is also the change in the concept of time. Here too we see again the fundamental relationship between dream and death. Already in dreams the wealth of what has been experienced often does not coincide with the earthly time that has elapsed, we think we have been dreaming for much longer. One of those questioned by Dr. Moody summarised the experience in the beyond, which went even further in this respect, in the sentence: "As soon as one has detached oneself from the earthly body, everything seems to speed up." This too is really self-evident and simply could not be otherwise. For owing to its faster intrinsic movement the ethereal soul-body is lighter, thus more permeable, and that brings with it an increased receptivity to experiencing. For everything that happens affects the spirit much more directly through the less dense covering. It is in a position to be able at the same time to grasp, that is to experience, much more than we can, because every happening can move the spirit much more directly. Here it is fundamentally a question of the same Law, which indeed we can also observe in the earthly: The more vibrations produced by the current with which we charge a cable, the more conversations we can simultaneously transmit along it; the higher the frequency of the light with which we take a photograph, the more detail it will show us. The laser-beam is the clearest example of this. In this increased ability to comprehend, which is characteristic of any faster movement, is found an easily verifiable explanation, based on the Laws of Nature, of the apparently so enigmatic saying "a thousand years are as one day".

But the altered feeling of time in the world beyond shows us very clearly that with regard to the concept of time we are under a misapprehension. We generally understand by it minutes, hours, days and years. Yet these are basically only a measure, derived from the movement of the earth in relation to the sun. We all know indeed that one hour does not equal another, that an hour of joy seems short to us, while one of pain seems like an eternity. Rich experiencing makes time pass as if on wings, while during inactive waiting it crawls by. Time is not the hour or the date, but the abundance of what we are able to experience, to accumulate in it. Hugo von Hofmannsthal expressed this very well when he said: "To the one who experiences, life expands." That is why it is so significant that, through the experience in the beyond of those who had briefly departed this life, this recognition is called to our consciousness and deepened. For it already means the first step towards answering the ever-repeated question about the purpose of our life. We realise that to live means to experience!

In this connection another experience which those who hovered between life and death were able to have gains special significance. For they experienced that in the world beyond only a completely different kind of knowledge counts. It was, as they described it, a deeper knowledge, a knowing as it were "with the soul", which is connected with the origins and interweavings of that which "holds the world together at its core". To acquire this kind of knowledge, as they were told by helpful beings in the beyond, is the most important thing, even already here on earth. And this should not only make us think, it should arouse us. For it certainly shows how wrong our education is, how much precious time in our life we spend on learning things which after all are quite unimportant. Here runs the dividing line between intellect and spirit. What we acquire by learning is of use to the intellect; stored in the cells of our brain it remains behind with our physical body. Only what we experience, perceive intuitively, what moves our spirit in this way, enters into us; that alone can we take with us. But today the whole of mankind suffers under the one-sided intellectual development. We accomplish splendid works of technology, but we lack the ability to control them, to use them wisely, because instead of letting ourselves be guided by the spirit we have left the guidance to the spirit's earthly instrument, the intellect. Thus everywhere we interfere in the natural happening, without being able to foresee the consequences, because we lack the true knowledge of the structure of this Creation. The deeply moving recognition of Goethe's Faust has unfortunately lost none of its validity even today:

"Oh happy he who can still hope to rise out of this flood of errors!

"What we do not know is just what we need to know, and what we know we cannot make use of!"

All who during the temporary withdrawal from their physical body had left the earthly world experienced the nearness of a loving light-being, who mediated to them a review of their earth-life. Entirely of themselves, they came to recognise thereby how much had been wrong in it, how much suffering they had caused others, often unknowingly, and how much time they had wasted. Some of them returned to earthly life with the greatest reluctance, and even remonstrated vehemently with their rescuers. But all who had been "over there" like that brought back with them the resolve to live differently, more consciously, in future.

And this I consider really the most important of what these

reports about life after death have to give us. For this review of life, the insight and the conclusions drawn from it, are surely the clear sign of a responsibility, a responsibility of which the spirit immediately becomes conscious as soon as it has laid aside the shackles of the earthly. For then its intellectual considerations of earthly expediency, then all its doubts have been automatically removed. But responsibility can never be an end in itself. It can only grow in connection with a task. Thus man has a task. But who is to tell us what it is?

It is just at this decisive point that we are let down by those books and writings which deal with life before this life and life after our death, let down by parapsychology and thanatology. Altogether they can tell us nothing more than that this earth-life is a passage in a further-reaching existence, but above all that death is not the end.

Certainly that in itself is extremely important. You have already heard how much easier even the mere knowledge of a continued life can one day make severance from the earthly body. But the importance of this knowledge goes even further. Once you have pushed open the gate to the wholeness of our existence your gaze will reach beyond this earth-life. You will not then feel yourselves totally bound up with the earthly like those who bind themselves to it of their own accord, through the belief that they would live only here and only once. Such an attitude in a human being brings forth its consequences at the time of death. For through this clinging to the earth the ethereal soul-body also becomes denser and thus heavier, because his wishes, directed towards the earth, need to be as close to the earth as possible. With this I am already going beyond what is contained in the reports compiled by Dr. Moody. But let us not forget that all these people were not actually dead. They had only temporarily left their earthly body for greater or lesser distances. When they gave an account of it they had already come back into this body, even though some of them actually may have died later. But at the time when they had the experiences described, the ethereal connection-cord of which I spoke earlier was not yet severed. All these descriptions therefore relate to an intermediate realm, a short-term transition. They do indeed confirm to us the existence of a "beyond", and of an extra-terrestrial life, but they tell us nothing about what happens to the soul after final severance from the earthly body, thus after the disintegration of the "silver cord". And here, in the interest of completing my explanations, I must still take this important next step. For all too easily the erroneous impression could otherwise arise that the beyond had only joyful things to offer to everyone. The fate of the ethereal "soul" after the final severance depends of course on the lightness or heaviness of the ethereal body. But we create its variation for ourselves through the aims we give to our desires. The higher they are in the rightly-understood spiritual sense, the lighter will our soul-body thereby become, and the baser they are the denser it will become. We can indeed experience ever again within us that gloomy thoughts "press us down", earthly worries "burden" us, make our heart "heavy", but a noble intuitive perception, a serene disposition, "uplift" us, make us "winged", and we "feel light at heart". These descriptions are certainly no empty illusion. They are the absolutely fitting description of a process in which the ethereal body participates very decisively, because every such stirring of our spirit, the intuitive perception, can only manifest in the earthly body by way of the ethereal body.

But the moment the cord which binds us here to our earthly body has disintegrated, this ethereal "soul" rises or falls in accordance with the Law of Gravitation familiar to us all. We know this Law as buoyancy, in water as Archimedes' Principle, but it manifests most clearly with gases. Any earthly substance, when it changes into a gaseous state, thus when it has become finer and lighter, as you must know, takes its place in accordance with the Law of Gravity. And through this Law heaven and hell are also explained, because it brings about a completely natural separation. For at the place to which the Law of Gravity automatically leads it, every soul will be surrounded by such souls as have the same weight and therefore essentially the same nature. This being together with their kind may be heaven for some, but for others – as long as they themselves do not bring about a change through a judicious transformation of their volition – it may be hell. –

But once we have grasped that after the falling away of the physical body, our stay is determined by the Law of Gravity, which automatically separates the homogeneous species at any given time, we shall have come another big step nearer the answer to the question of the meaning of our life. For we will then recognise that this, our earthly body, is a mantle, a protective wall which – like a diving-bell through its weight – holds us fast in the gross material substance of this earth-world, thereby making it possible for human beings of the most diverse character to live together and side by side. Hence the Earth is a reservoir, a meeting-point for what otherwise would have to remain separate. I will speak about the significance of this fact later.

Thus you see: To become clear about death really means first to occupy oneself rightly with life. Dag Hammerskjöld, the late Secretary-General of the United Nations, expressed this very aptly. He said:

"If we go to the root of the matter, it is our concept of death that decides our answers to all the questions which life poses."

But does not this statement already make one recognise how helpless are even those who think seriously? Even if we know that this life is only harnessed between the poles of the before and the after, nevertheless we are living here and now, and here and now we need to be clear about where the answers to the questions of life are to be found.

You may ask: Then what do we have religions for? On the part of their bringers, the teachings were all in fact originally adapted to be a support to us, and lead to the Truth they held in common. But because from the very beginning they were not passed on in written form, misunderstandings have flowed into them. The personal ability to comprehend of those who passed anything on has always changed something in the teaching, narrowed it down. In the course of centuries the content was eventually adapted more and more to human wishes, and the picture was arranged as we would like to see it. May I, for instance, perhaps remind you that the so decisively important doctrine of reincarnation, of rebirth as a human being, through which indeed the Love and Justice of God first become intelligible to us human spirits, was only expunged from Christian creeds by a very small majority decision at the Council of Constantinople in the year 553.

And now do please reflect: If at that time only a few men had decided differently, reincarnation would be a matter of course also for Western humanity. There would then be no need to battle against walls of doubt and of prejudice, to free our thinking from that dreadful constraint into which it has fallen solely through this unhappy decision, which has robbed us of the outlook on the connections and the vastness of our existence. So you see even from this one example:

Man has presumed to decide what is allowed to be true! Hence the inconsistencies and gaps which prevent so many thinking people from accepting the tenets of faith in their entirety. But Truth must convince as a whole. In face of it there can be no reservations.

What is left for us of all the wise teachings are admonitions and rules of conduct. Most of these are of high moral value. But they lack that cohesion which could form a world-picture from them, a world-picture that is able to give us the answer to those questions which we simply cannot evade. They are:
1. the question of the purpose of our existence,
2. and that of how we can fulfil such a purpose.

You may smile, and think to yourselves: Nothing else then? I am fully aware that the most eminent thinkers have at all times racked their brains over this. But what has come of it? In many cases only conflicting philosophical dogmas aimed at proving the intellectual sophistry of their founding fathers, rather than giving genuine vital help. Yet I dare to assert that the answers are by no means so difficult to find; nor are they so intricate and complicated as it appears to us. For all Truth is basically simple. It is just in simplicity, which is a result of the uniformity of the whole, that true greatness lies. We do know today – to mention only a few examples – that the immense variety of plants, animals and human beings has its foundation in the same four genetic building-stones, that the cells in plant, animal and man are built up in the same way, that every cell, in whatever organ it may be located, always contains the master-plan of the whole; we know that arms, legs, wings and fins have issued from the same fundamental design; we know that the same forces are at work within an atom as between the solar systems. Does this not teach us that everything is based on uniform Laws? That only the variation in their effects causes the multiplicity that seems confusing to us?

What we need therefore is the overall perspective. Hence I must again speak of the Grail Message "In the Light of Truth". It would lead too far if we were to enter here into the significance of the Holy Grail. Our mental image of it is linked with the concept of something sublime, sacred. May this suffice to allow us to perceive the Origin of that helpful

Call which has therewith gone out to mankind, and to mediate to us a faint idea of the loftiness of this view, which lies incomparably far above all that is offered to us in other descriptions of the beyond. Therefore indeed the Author could say:

"I wish to fill the gaps which have hitherto remained unanswered in the souls of men, and which will never leave any serious thinker in peace if he is honestly seeking for the Truth."

I have used a few points of what is stated in the Grail Message as the basis of the explanation about the nature of death and the process of dying. But this Message contains and tells us much more. It not only takes from us the fear of death, it takes from us – which is much more important – the fear of life. If you occupy yourselves with this Work you will experience the rightness of the sentence, the significance of which simply cannot be plumbed, which outlines the content of this Work and states:

"With my Message I now open the Book of Creation for you!"

As you will surely understand, I cannot within the compass of a lecture unfold before you a world-picture of such immense breadth, which also shows our path in this Creation. I must continue to confine myself to what is most important. It seems to me, as already mentioned, that this most important factor is the question of the purpose of our life. It is on account of this that so many human beings despair, since they can find no answer. They escape into excesses, into the sham world of drugs, throw themselves into the arms of the false teachings of religious impostors, or thoughtlessly hazard this life, which to them appears meaningless and therefore worthless; indeed they even throw it away.

But does not even a glance into this Creation tell us that everything in it has a purpose? Ecology, the science of natural co-operation, indeed reveals to us how one thing gears into the other, completing and furthering one another. In this interplay of the great household of Creation, everything fulfils the role assigned to it. How then could we assume that just man is without function in this system?

But every search for the purpose of life, if it does not reach purely nihilistic conclusions, is in danger of moving only in abstract ideas. Yet we do not want to lose the ground under our feet. This is not at all necessary for us, because even the greatest is always reflected in the small, and everything in which lies the great Truth of this Creation is already around us here in images. You will surely have already noticed that I have referred again and again to experiences familiar to us all, or to recognitions of the natural sciences. I do so because you are meant to learn from this that the processes with which we are here concerned run their course according to exactly the same Laws.

I said earlier that the core of man, his real ego, is spirit. Now in that part of the text which I have brought to your attention in order to clarify this concept, it was said that the spiritual world lies higher and forms the upper, lightest part of Creation. What therefore have we, as spiritual creatures, to do here in the earthly?

The inadequacy of our institutions, of our human activity, already bears the answer within it: Man is not a fully developed spirit. His spirit-core is a seed-grain, a spiritual germ. Like every seed-grain it contains the full potentialities of its species, but gradual ripening is required for them.

What does Nature do to enable the seed of a plant to ripen? It is rooted into the earth. The manifold forces thereby working on it advance and strengthen it.

Now consider: The Creator has done likewise with us. We are sunk into this earthly world as seed-grains. Only the species distinguishes us from the ripening of the plant. We are in the World of Matter for the maturing of our own species, the spirit. The earthly experiencing with its constant need to overcome difficulties caused by material substance – just think for instance of the proverb, "the spirit is willing, but the flesh is weak" – is meant to help us to recognise the power of the spirit within us, and to strengthen it for conscious activity. How significant it is, in view of the fundamental uniformity of the Laws of Nature, that even physically we need friction with material substance in order to move step by step, to progress. And only here, in the mantle of this dense-material corporeality, is it also possible, as I have said earlier, for human beings of different levels of spiritual maturity to be able to live together on the same plane. That, however, offers us a diversity of experience like nowhere in other spheres. And it is this diversity of experience that facilitates the ability to mature, and makes earth-life so important.

But where is this development ultimately to lead us? The answer is supplied by our nature: To the Spiritual Realm that corresponds to our species, but to which we can only attain in a fully-matured state.

Just consider, please, the structure of Creation. Let us begin right away with ourselves: The organelles in every cell are independent industries, but at the same time part of the wholeness of the cell, which in turn is part of the tissues. The tissues form organs, which in their turn are part of groups of organs. These finally make up the body. Man for his part is an independent creature, and yet part of the family; this is part of a group which by way of the village, the people, the race, finally embraces the whole of mankind. Everything is embedded in this hierarchical gradation-order, which in the material world reaches from the elementary particles to atoms and molecules, right up to the celestial bodies, the solar systems, the galaxies.

Now in this structure we find everywhere the double function of all that exists, namely to be an independent whole and also part of a greater order. This involves two apparently conflicting necessities: Self-assertion of the individual whole, and at the same time its fitting into, integrating with a greater unit. In this connection I would like to quote to you from the most recent book of the scientist-philosopher Arthur Koestler*. He writes:

* "Der Mensch – Irrläufer der Evolution", Scherz-Verlag Bern/Munich

"The constellation Self-assertion versus Integration... exists in biology, psychology, ecology, and wherever we encounter complex hierarchical systems, thus practically everywhere we look: In the living animal or the living plant each part must assert its individuality just as in the social system, because otherwise the organism would lose its structure and disintegrate.

"But at the same time each part must bow to the demand of the whole. In a healthy organism and a healthy society the two tendencies are balanced at all levels of the hierarchy."

Herein lies the confirmation of what is shown to us in the Grail Message. Just as it is for everything earthly, so it applies to us also, to fit ourselves into the community at every stage of our spiritual development, with the spiritual abilities we have so far developed, and as personality. Quite a few people believe that the final goal of our path is Nirvana, the complete dissolution of our ego into an all-embracing power. The mistaken idea that the ego is something deserving of destruction could only arise because here, on this low earthly plane, we know it for the most part only as selfishness, as egotism. But what has Koestler to say on that point: "In a healthy organism and a healthy society the two tendencies are balanced at all levels of the hierarchy." Therefore let us not derive the task assigned to us in the order of Creation from the faulty current state, but from the healthy desired state. From this it follows that the goal of our existence can lie only in co-operating with the mechanism of this Creation as a fully matured spirit, while remaining personal. The more conscious we become on this path to it, the easier, of course, it comes to us to fit in, since we recognise increasingly that this order of Creation is so perfect that co-operating in service therein means at the same time the greatest personal advantage. Out of a free volition we are then prepared to help in the realisation of the great order, because it holds happiness for us personally.

If for once we fully grasp this inwardly, it must become clear to us that there can be nothing more beautiful for the human spirit than voluntary service. For "voluntary" means unhindered by ties – which have to be spoken of later – means being allowed to follow one's own volition, thus to act out of innermost conviction. This freedom of will alone frees the concept of serving from the association of slavish subjection to an alien will, frees it also from the appearance of spiritual passivity. It is a joyfully active, conscious serving, being of use to a more comprehensive purpose lying outside our own person. Certainly, this longing to be of use lies deeply rooted in each one of us. Is it not the worst thing for the unemployed, for the old, to see no task before them, to be no more needed? This indeed reveals how much our spirit longs to fulfil its mission!

The matured homecoming to the source of our species, to the high, luminous World of the Spirit, is thus the individually personal goal which is set for each one of us. But at the same time there follows from this at every level the task for the community. For man, equipped with the core of a higher species imbued with the urge to develop, is here already enabled and called to be the connecting-link between the material worlds and the Spiritual Realm. He is meant to form the bridge by which, uplifting and ennobling, the beauty and harmony of that higher world flows down into the earthly. True art, which outlives the ages, is an example of the fulfilment of this task. –

And is it not remarkable that, undeterred by all baseness, disregarding all the dreadful things which in the course of his history man has done and still does to man, the concept of humanity for us is nevertheless still associated with the idea of love for our neighbour, dignity and noble-mindedness. For this embryonically traced image of the higher purpose of man's existence, towards which he has to develop, is indestructibly imprinted on the human spirit.

Now we have indeed found the answer to the question of the purpose of our life. But it still remains for us to clarify how we can achieve its realisation.

For there in truth lies our human problem: We know hardly anything of that great order which must become joyfully self-evident to us. And the guilt for this lies with us. Creation itself is the language in which the Creator speaks to us. But just as a child must learn the language of his parents in order to know what they want of him, and what he must do, so man has to strive to understand the language of Creation.

Therefore, the Author of the Grail Message calls to us:

"Learn to understand Creation aright in its Laws! Therein lies the way upwards to the Light!"

Even just looking up at the starry firmament teaches us that the planets trace their course in accordance with unchangeable – and only because of this calculable for us – Laws. Here, in the Laws which order and uphold all that exists, and which indeed surround also us here on all sides, we meet with the infallible support which we must find lacking everywhere else. How then could we still doubt the rightness of the sentence contained in the Grail Message:

"The man who knows Creation in its lawful activity will soon understand the sublime Will of God in it also."

And to recognise just this Will of God is indispensable for us. But is it not strange: In our criminal code we lay down that ignorance of the law is no protection from punishment. That is to say: He who transgresses the existing norms has to take the consequences in any case. It is his fault if he has not troubled to acquaint himself with the laws.

And to mention only one example, even if we authorise someone to drive a motor vehicle we require him to pass a test to prove his knowledge of the relevant laws, because in our opinion he would otherwise be a danger to himself and others.

Indeed how sensible, how judicious we are in these matters! Does it not occur to us then that the Creator, too, might be as wise as we are, and that the same principle might apply also to us with regard to the Laws of this Creation?

But how have we acted up till now? We have left it to the

scientists to concern themselves with these Laws, because we have regarded them as Laws of Nature. At best they have interested us only insofar as we could make use of them technically. But we have omitted to draw lessons from them for ourselves as spiritual creatures. The physicist Walter Heitler, Professor at the University of Zurich*, also holds the same view: "But the time is indeed ripe for us to begin to be aware of the metaphysical questions concealed behind the Laws of Nature."

Our knowledge has doubled in the last three decades alone. Specialist fields are beginning to merge, a great unity is becoming apparent. Here and there we already find the beginnings of a thinking of wholeness. More and more we recognize the rightness of the sentence long since written in the Grail Message: "Indeed everything in Creation works reciprocally." Even scientists now speak of an "intermeshed" world. We can no longer act as though this network had nothing to do with us. We are interwoven with it, not only bodily-physically but also in our human-spiritual existence, because the continuous validity of all the Laws of Creation does not stop short of us. Only the outworking of these Laws affects at one time the earthly, then the ethereal or the spiritual, always according to the species concerned.

Modern physics is on the way to recognising this. Its most eminent representatives, such as Bohr, Heisenberg, Pauli and others, perceive for example in the complementary principle – in the fact that the minutest particles of matter behave at times

* "Man and Science" published by Oliver and Boyd, 1963

like solid bodies but at other times like waves, thus like something intangible – a correspondence to the relationship between body and spirit. This culminates in the statement that this dual nature of man reflects the dual nature of the fundamental building-stones of the Universe, or vice versa. Thus the application of the lawfulness of Nature to the spiritual seems to be quite permissible also according to the ideas of science. We have even known of this uniformity for a long time; we have only forgotten it. You must all be familiar with the well-known words of truth: "As the seed, so is the harvest"; "As you make your bed, so must you lie in it"; "Take heed or take the consequences". All these are nothing other than the abbreviation of an experience which man has had with the Law of Reciprocal Action, one of the most important and fundamental Laws of Creation. No one would dispute that the metaphors used also contain a figurative meaning, thus that material and spiritual happenings have here been quite consciously equated.

Only a few decades ago it was recognised that this lawfulness even has a much more far-reaching significance. For in it lies also a self-regulating factor which ultimately provides for the maintenance of an unchangeable order.

Norbert Wiener, who was the first to make possible the technical application of this principle, coined for it the term cybernetics, derived from the Greek word "kybernetes", which means much the same as "helmsman". It was clear to him that in the machines he invented, the computers, he was reproducing modes of action which are characteristic of living creatures. He therefore also called his book "Cybernetics, or the Transfer of Information in Living Creatures and Machines". But he had not considered that everything that takes place in living creatures is simply a lawfulness of what is living. And what could be more living than this Creation as a whole, which from the greatest to the smallest is full of ceaseless movement. Thus it was gradually realised that these automatic regulating-processes are to be found everywhere, that they are inherent not only throughout the household of Nature, but inevitably also in human institutions; indeed they even determine historical and economic processes, social structures, sport, language, the judicial system and inter-human relationships. In short, there is nothing which could not be traced back to the working of this automatic regulating, quite simply because everything has issued from the vitality of this Creation, and through it alone can continue to exist. Thus we have before us a fundamental Law of the whole mechanism of Creation, and with it an excellent opportunity of illustrating what it means to get to know Creation in its Laws. You will see how many fundamental questions are answered in them.

We make use of cybernetic lawfulness in all kinds of automatic devices and control computers, without which our present way of life can hardly be imagined. Thus you need not be a technician to understand the governing principle present in it. For whether you now preset the desired temperature on your refrigerator or central heating, select a certain program for your washing-machine or dish-washer, or whether an electronic brain combines a mass of data to maintain a pre-arranged target, it is only a question of the order of magnitude, but not of the principle. You are surely aware that such equipment has to be "programmed". Here as there the essence of the principle consists in

a) absolute
b) optimum

realisation of this "program", in that all influences interfering with the course of the program release an automatic reaction, which in turn eliminates the interference. And now, ladies and gentlemen, let us apply this principle, which as stated can be encountered in all kinds of processes, and which has only been technically imitated by us, to the whole of Creation. Do not the Natural Laws, which we can only discover and take note of but not change, then appear to us as the "program" according to which everything that takes place in this mechanism of Creation runs its course? But whence comes this program? Surely it does not arise of itself; as we know, there must be a "programmer". Must not the Creator then appear to us as the One Who drew up this program and fed it into Creation? And you see: When a person programs a control computer he does so according to his will, that is he feeds his will into it in the form of the "program". The world-mechanism operating in accordance with the same Laws of automatic control therefore bears within it the Will of God; it is HIS Will which appears to us as Natural Law.

Please bear in mind at this point that it is part of the essence of automatic control-mechanisms to guarantee the best possible end-result. If we succeed in doing so with a computer, must we not then – applying it to the great picture – all the more conclude that this was possible also for the Creator? Hence that the Laws of Creation or of Nature provide for the best possible? But this opens up to us an entirely new, immense focal point: For the best, the optimal, is of course the highest attainable, and thus perfection. In these Laws of Nature therefore the Perfection of God reveals Itself. By It their immovability also is explained. For what is perfect cannot be improved. Any change could only be for the worse. Therefore wherever we try to correct this perfection we experience setbacks.

But does not this also show us how wrong our picture of God has been up till now? There is no room for the concept of the old gentleman who would allow himself to be moved by our pleading and begging to dispense leniency or favour. The picture of HIM which this World unmistakably holds out is incomparably greater, more powerful and sublime than that which our little human thinking could conceive. God's Omnipotence therefore does not consist in arbitrary proceedings which we associate with the idea of power; it is the all-embracing Power which, because of its immovable Perfection, in the long run nothing can resist.

But this Creation-wide basic Law of automatic control, which seeks to eliminate every disturbance, also explains the concept of fate. It is the balancing reaction to that which we ourselves have brought into being. Here too we see that ignorance of the Laws does not protect us from the consequences, but insight into the error comes to us more easily if we have not committed it consciously. We need not move within the abstract at all in these considerations, for we find examples of this in all natural happenings. If for instance you decide to run a 100 metre race, you cannot prevent yourself from panting when you have reached the goal. Through the exertion of running you have reduced the optimum supply of air for your body-household, and now this automatically enforces the balance. You only need to alter the scale of this example within the framework of the Creation-wide Laws of control to find the answer to the question of man's free will and his fate. As these control-Laws demonstrate to us, we are certainly free to make decisions, but we are bound to their consequences. Yet since in the course of our existence – here I am deliberately not speaking only of this earth-life – we have already made countless decisions, whose consequences do not always come about as instantaneously as in the example quoted earlier, we often find ourselves bound, constrained by some inescapable pressure of such reactions. We then doubt the freedom of will, and speak of dependence, of fate. But what appears to us as such because of its inevitability is nothing other than the reaction of our own intuitive perception, thought and deed, which is "sent" to us to make up for what we have confused and entangled in the great order of Creation. With a piece of string too you can only untie a knot by pulling it back through the loop through which it was formed. Therefore suicide is never a way out of existing difficulties either; for it does not exempt the one concerned from the need to undo the self-made knots. Rather it burdens him with the additional guilt of having disregarded the gift of being allowed to mature. For the inequity that seems to us like punishment has ultimately a much wider meaning: It is an appeal to our reason, with the aim of leading us back on to what for us is the only right path, which to our detriment we were about to forsake. Thus it is a matter of a solicitous nudge to correct our course. In this reciprocal action, which brings to each what he himself has released, at the same time lie inseparably united the Justice and the Love of God. HE has done HIS part from the very beginning, by placing His Will, Which also provides what is best for us, in this Creation as Law. It is up to us at last to make the most of the opportunities thereby granted to us, for *therein* lies God's ever-present Grace, which we have only to seize.

It is just this immovable automatic working of the Laws of Creation, the helps lying ever ready for us in them, but also the necessities arising from them for us, which the Grail Message "In the Light of Truth" describes and explains. The discovery of automatic control techniques, of cybernetics, has confirmed the rightness of these explanations, and therewith also the significance of the following sentence from the Grail Message:

"Only the man who lives in the Laws of God is free!"

The reasoning has now become understandable to us: Only such a man, as the Law of Automatic Reciprocal Action teaches us, can avoid painful reactions which restrict his freedom of will, and partake fully of the help that lies in the Laws of God. Therefore also Jesus, Who from His Origin was Himself a Part of the Truth contained in these immovable Laws, was able to say not only: "I *am* . . . the Truth and the Life," but also: "He that is not with me is against me;" because everything that does not fit in with these Laws disturbs the continuous "running of the program" of this Creation.

Therefore these Laws also allow us to recognise that we may not continue indefinitely being an unthinking disturber of the great harmony of Creation. Ecological processes, which of course take place in accordance with the same Laws, demonstrate clearly that a wrong development once begun goes on ever faster, finally driving to a point where catastrophe is unavoidable. Some years ago leading scientists hinted at this in their report to the "Club of Rome". And how do we do things in our educational systems? We allow a pupil who has not reached the required standard to resit examinations, even to repeat the class. But one day there comes an end to these opportunities for someone who does not know how to make use of them. The target set must be reached within a definite time. Were it not so it would only mean the encouragement of laziness and unwillingness to learn. Let us not consider the Creator as less wise than ourselves, who can only imitate what already exists in Creation! We too are given the opportunity through reincarnation, rebirth, to make up for mistakes which we have made in the Material World, and which therefore have also to be redeemed again here. That we are unable to remember earlier lives with our day-consciousness – I mention this only in passing – is not at all important. For the day-conscious recollection is formed through the storage of proteins in our brain. But this brain disintegrates with physical death. What we have experienced, however, what has formed us, has entered into our spirit; it constitutes our inclinations, our abilities, in short our personality, with which we enter into a new life, or better expressed carry on our existence. But – and here may I return after this short digression to what I said earlier – everything points to the fact that we do not have unlimited time for judicious learning. Viewed thus, it appears significant that the meeting of the "Club of Rome" which took place in June 1979 in Salzburg was concerned with the need to study the Creation-wide connections without which the continued existence of humanity would seem to be in jeopardy. But with this an immense circle closes, the beyond and this world unite for the same Call. For this same admonition was also given to those who had already briefly glimpsed the beyond, and it coincides with the words already quoted from the Grail Message:

"Learn to understand Creation aright in its Laws!"

For these Laws are not a sophisticated system of thought such as theology and philosophy offer us, but immovable, indisputable living reality. Through them – and only through them – can that which with cryptic ambiguity is generally called "belief" become conviction for us, because this belief is daily confirmed through the Laws of this Creation. Thus we find also as the first sentence in the Grail Message the words which hold out to every seeker the best that can happen to him:

"The bandage falls, and belief becomes conviction!"

This is a completely new note in matters of belief. A note to which our ear should be particularly receptive just at this time, when the confusion caused by our lack of understanding is everywhere recoiling upon us; for how else could we still find the way out?

To many a person this automatic irrevocability of the Laws may seem hard, indeed even frightening, because – in our own interest – they are demanding. But do we not all know the proverbial words of wisdom: "The mills of God grind slowly, yet they grind exceeding small"?

What is described here as "the mills of God" is surely nothing other than the Natural Law of Reciprocal Action, and the certain arrival of the reciprocal action testifies to its irrevocability. The discovery of the technique of automatic control and its application to the whole of Creation therefore only confirm in modern technical guise an ancient empirical knowledge. It tells us that this application likewise to extra-material happenings is not only permissible, but also right.

But this fundamentally loving severity is at the same time also a criterion of the seriousness with which you yourselves approach these questions. For here it is a matter of deciding:

Do you wish to form God according to your image, or to pay attention to HIS Will? The Author of the Grail Message has therefore written even in his preface:

"I am addressing earnest seekers only."

Of you who have followed my explanations on fundamental questions of our existence may I assume that there is this earnestness.

I can well imagine that you still have many a question. In the course of this lecture I could only enter into very little. But the Grail Message presents the answers far better than I could. It is a Work – I would like emphatically to stress this, because I have been repeatedly asked about it – which in spite of its alleged similarity with the *basic* truths of other teachings cannot be co-ordinated with any of these, even from the mere fact that the revealing of the connections here reaches incomparably further. Therefore do not imagine that you could begin anywhere, because you perhaps think that you have already heard this or that. There is a structure in the Book which imperceptibly, but from the very beginning, leads you into a new kind of seeing and experiencing. You will perhaps ask yourselves why I refer ever again to the Grail Message. I will tell you quite frankly the reason, for you are not to think you have come to a propaganda meeting. Again and again I experience, in private as well as in my profession as a lawyer, how helplessly people face the questions of life, how they torment themselves for an explanation of one thing or another, and in the end resign themselves to thinking that probably it must be that we cannot arrive at a satisfactory answer. You yourselves may well have had similar experiences. Therefore if as a seeker one has had the inestimable good fortune to come upon this Message, then quite simply I consider it one's human duty to bring it to the attention of other seekers. For here, in penetratingly clear language, understandable to all, lies the help for our needs, the answer to our questions. But I can assure you that whether you acquire this book, whether you read it or not, neither I nor anyone else has anything to gain. Nor – and unfortunately today this must be emphatically stressed – will any sect seek to win you. You alone are to draw benefit from this Work. Only when you have recognised its value will people to whom the same has happened be prepared to help you deepen your insights insofar as you wish it.

But in any case there is still something you would like to hear from me. The name of the Author, which so far I have not mentioned. His name was Oskar Ernst Bernhardt, but he wrote this Work under the name Abd-ru-shin. I have purposely not mentioned his name until now; for to be honest, what use is this knowledge to you? When Jesus once walked the earth He had no other proof than His Word, than the Message that He brought. He, the simple son of a carpenter from Nazareth, could not lay claim to any "prominence". Those who followed Him had to recognise Him by the importance of His Teaching. Thus the Author of this Work also wrote:

"Heed not the Bringer, but the Word!"

If we consider it aright, ladies and gentlemen, this sentence contains enormously much. It brings something very different from the dim endeavours which nowadays are only too often to be found under the pretext of spiritual enlightenment. A true helper will never make his person the centre of his teaching. More I would not like to say to you on this subject now. Otherwise I would rob you of an irretrievable experience of joy that awaits you with the serious study of this Work.

With this study you set foot on the path to a conscious life. For as long as we are ignorant of our human spiritual nature, as long as we do not know our path and goal, then no matter how intellectually clever and learned we may be we are in truth blind and deaf. Unconscious of our own power and its interplay with the powers of this Creation, we move apathetically along, physically alive indeed but spiritually dead. Only with the recognition that we are interwoven in the working of Creation do we, do things around us visibly come to life, for the word of the Grail Message comes true:

"You can immediately recognise that you really have the Word of Truth in my Message if you look around you wakefully; for your whole earth-life up till now, as well as the new experiencing of every moment, both outwardly and inwardly, will become completely clear to you as soon as you illumine and regard it from my Message."

I hope I have succeeded in opening your eyes at least to a very small but extremely important section of the vitality of this Creation, and at the same time also to the vastness of our existence. Although we began with death we end with life, with – I hope – a more conscious life. Thus I would like to take leave of you with that sentence with which the Bringer of the Grail Message closed his Foreword. It is the sentence which embraces our entire human task, reaching far beyond this earth-life, and which I would like to give you as my wish:

"See that you are truly alive in the wonderful Creation of your God!"

THE GRAIL MESSAGE
"IN THE LIGHT OF TRUTH"

The Grail Message of Abd-ru-shin mediates the knowledge of the upbuilding of Creation. In simple words it explains the connections without a gap, and gives a complete survey of all the activity in Creation.

It is directed solely to the individual human being, irrespective of creed, nationality or race, because it is he alone who has to bear the responsibility for everything he thinks and does.

Surely and unswervingly it shows him the way he has to follow in order to find true happiness even here on earth, which means to attain inner peace and joyful activity.

The root of all evil, of present and past afflictions and distress, lies only with the *individual* human being. If *he* turns earnestly towards the good, everything else also becomes good. It has an immediate effect upon marriage, upon the family, and finally also upon the entire people, which can only then develop its *own* characteristics and its *own* culture to the highest degree.

In the Grail Message detailed explanations are given as to what the free will of man really is, what intellect and intuitive perception, soul and spirit signify, their tasks and their relation to each other.

The three great Laws of Creation – the Law of Reciprocal

Action (the Law of Sowing and Reaping), the Law of the Attraction of Homogeneous Species, and the Law of Gravitation – are explained in all their greatness and simplicity.

Thus we learn, for instance, that the Law of Sowing and Reaping (Galatians 6, 7) not only applies to the earthly seed, but also to man's actions and thoughts, which through the working of the incorruptible Laws of Creation ripen into fruits, corresponding exactly to good or evil volition, of which man alone must taste. Thoughts, intuitive perceptions and deeds are very effective forms or "works" (Revelation 14, 13) that remain connected with their author until he severs himself from them. They form his "fate", and sometimes he is struck by "blows of fate" which he cannot account for, although the cause of these was given by *him* in former earth-lives.

It is repeatedly emphasised in the Grail Message how important to man is the knowledge of the Laws of Creation, for the very reason that his spirit possesses the ability to recognise the Will of God in these Laws. A true upbuilding is only possible if man bases his entire earth-life on the Laws of Creation. Thereby he fulfils the Will of God.

We must take these Laws as they are, unchangeable and eternal, always the same, just as God, Who has woven them into Creation, is always the Same, the Eternal One.

Further important questions that move the seeking man are dealt with clearly and objectively, whether they concern fate, hereditary sin, the meaning and purpose of life, birth and death, the beyond, incarnation, the sexual problem, marriage; or the Mission of Christ and His death on the Cross, the Son of God and the Son of Man, the mystery of Lucifer, the Last Judgement, the Cosmic Turning-Point, the Holy Grail, the Grail Castle.

As regards the Grail Castle, Abd-ru-shin says that it really exists at the summit of the *spiritual* Creation, far above the Paradise of the human spirits, as the focal point and point of transformation of the radiations which come from the Divine Sphere above for the lower-lying parts of Creation. In the Revelation of John the Grail Castle is called "the Temple of God" (Revelation 11, 19).

Only from this height can an unbroken, comprehensive view over the entire working of Creation be given in a Message from the Grail. Hence the name "Grail Message", which in addition receives special significance because it appears at a time when mankind stands at an important turning-point.

It is self-evident that a Grail Message stands absolutely on the ground of Christ's teaching. It merely takes into consideration the fact that the man of today has so trained his intellectual thinking, has so keenly sharpened his instruments for thinking, that the childlike simple belief which Jesus demanded at that time no longer suffices for him to be able to follow the way to God. For that reason the Grail Message explains Christ's teaching in a language adapted to man's present way of thinking. Thus a knowledge is mediated to him giving him that certainty out of which, in place of belief, there gradually grows the conviction necessary today.

An example of this is given here from the lecture "Ascent"

from Volume I: "And so it must rise steadily upwards towards the longed-for Light. An evil volition presses the spirit down and makes it heavy, whereas a good volition uplifts it.

"For this, too, Jesus has already shown you the simple way leading unerringly to the goal; for deep truth lies in the simple words: '*Love thy neighbour as thyself!*'

"With these words He gave the key to freedom and ascent! Because it is an irrefutable fact: What you do for your neighbour you do in reality only for yourselves! Solely for yourselves, since according to the Eternal Laws everything returns to you without fail, good or evil, either already here or there. It will surely come! Thus you are shown the simplest of ways in which this step to the good volition is to be understood.

"You should give to your neighbour with your *being*, your nature! Not necessarily with money and goods. For then those without means would be excluded from the possibility of giving. And in this being, in this 'giving yourself' in the relation with your neighbour, in the consideration and respect you voluntarily offer him, lies the 'love' of which Jesus speaks; lies also the help you give to your neighbour, because it enables him to change himself or ascend further, because he gains strength from it."

Abd-ru-shin, the Author of the Grail Message, writes:

"The hearer and reader of my lectures should always work within himself, keenly probing and building bridges from one lecture to the other, as well as out into the great and small world happenings! Only then will he be able to understand the Grail Message and find that it gradually shapes itself into one complete whole, without leaving any gaps. Again and again in all the happenings the reader will come back to the basic features. He can explain everything and deduce everything without having to change even one single sentence . . . The Word of the Grail Message lives, so that it permits only those people who really carry the honest desire in their souls to find abundantly! All else is automatically rejected by it. For the arrogant and those who only seek superficially the Message will remain the book with seven seals!"

In the Light of Truth

The Grail Message by Abd-ru-shin

Among all books of spiritual content this Work occupies a unique place. It brings the recognition of the all-embracing Laws of Creation, and guides the reader to a profound knowledge of the meaning of existence.

The Author writes:
"... I wish to fill the gaps which have so far always remained unanswered in the souls of men, and which never leave any serious thinker in peace, if he honestly seeks for the Truth."

Edition in three Volumes:
Linen
Volume I 212 pages
Volume II 414 pages
Volume III 458 pages

Edition in one Volume:
Linen 1062 pages

Special edition:
India paper,
leather 1062 pages

Original edition: German

Translations available:
English
French
Italian
Dutch
Portuguese
Spanish
Czech

In preparation: Russian

The Grail Message "In the Light of Truth" contains the following lectures:

Further writings by Abd-ru-shin:

The Ten Commandments of God and the Lord's Prayer	linen	72 pages
Questions and Answers	linen	232 pages
Prayers	staple-bound	12 pages

The Pocket Book Series:

Volume 1	*The World, as it could be!*	paperback	144 pages
Volume 2	*Knowledge for the World of Tomorrow!*	paperback	116 pages
Volume 3	*What lies behind it...!*	paperback	120 pages
Volume 4	*From the Heart of Africa*	paperback	108 pages
Volume 5	*A Gate Opens*	paperback	124 pages

Further publications:

A Gate Opens, Composite Volume	linen	394 pages
Helping Words	in paper cover	44 pages
The Apocalypse Today	staple-bound	16 pages
How are Things to Continue in these Times of Confusion and Affliction?	staple-bound	32 pages
How is it that we Live after Death and What is the Meaning of Life	in paper cover	68 pages
Hidden Connections Determine our Earth-life	in paper cover	44 pages

Please request leaflet from

Australia	**The Grail Movement of Australia** **Kalorama Chalet, Falls Road** **Kalorama, Vic. 3766**
Canada	**Grail Movement of Canada** **C.P. 277. Shawinigan, Québec, G9N 6T9**
Great Britain	**The Grail Foundation of Great Britain** **23, Hamilton Road, Sidcup, Kent**
India	**Representative in India:** **Kanayo F. Nwanze** **c/o P.O. Box 85, Khairatabad** **Hyderabad 500 004 A.P.**
Nigeria	**Grail Movement – Nigeria,** **Grailland, Iju Hill, P.O. Box 4157** **Lagos**
U.S. America	**Grail Foundation of America** **2081 Partridge Lane, Binghamton,** **N.Y. 13903**

STIFTUNG GRALSBOTSCHA
STUTTGA

9783878602392